Alvan Bond

A Historical Discourse

Alvan Bond

A Historical Discourse

ISBN/EAN: 9783741186585

Manufactured in Europe, USA, Canada, Australia, Japa

Cover: Foto ©ninafisch / pixelio.de

Manufactured and distributed by brebook publishing software
(www.brebook.com)

Alvan Bond

A Historical Discourse

A

HISTORICAL DISCOURSE,

DELIVERED AT THE

HUNDREDTH ANNIVERSARY

OF THE ORGANIZATION OF THE

SECOND CONGREGATIONAL CHURCH,

NORWICH, CONN., JULY 24, 1860.

WITH AN

APPENDIX.

BY ALVAN BOND, D. D.

NORWICH:
MANNING, PLATT & CO., PRINTERS, FRANKLIN SQUARE.
1860.

Norwich, July 26th, 1860.

Rev. ALVAN BOND, D. D.

DEAR SIR:

The undersigned Committee, appointed by the Second Congregational Church in relation to their Centennial Celebration, beg leave to express, for the Church and themselves, their hearty thanks for your excellent Historical Discourse on that occasion, and to request a copy of the same for publication.

WILLIAM WILLIAMS,
JOHN A. ROCKWELL,
GEORGE PERKINS,
EBENEZER LEARNED,
FRANCIS A. DORRANCE,
S. H. GROSVENOR,
CHARLES JOHNSON,
C. B. WEBSTER,
DAVID SMITH.

Norwich, July 27th, 1860.

GENTLEMEN:

Please accept my thanks for your note of yesterday, and for the kind manner in which you speak of the Historical Discourse, delivered on occasion of the Centennial Anniversary of our Church. In response to your request, it is submitted to your disposal for publication.

Sincerely Yours,

ALVAN BOND.

Messrs. WILLIAM WILLIAMS, and others.

HISTORICAL DISCOURSE.

BRETHREN AND FRIENDS:

The record of a hundred years in the history of our Church closes to-day. We have assembled to review this record, to revive the reminiscences of the past, and devoutly recognize in prayer and song the good hand of our God, as revealed to our Fathers in the way in which he led them.

The ecclesiastical vine which they planted in this rugged soil, has, amidst alternations of sunshine and storm, matured from weakness to a healthy, vigorous development, and promises to bring forth fruit in old age. Already " she hath sent out her boughs unto the sea, and her branches unto the river." On the hundredth anniversary of this century plant we come together, to sit and commune under her shadow, and render her the tribute of grateful affection, as we rehearse what our fathers have told us of the work of God in their days, in the times of old.

A hundred years does not, indeed, produce a very perceptible change in the progress of the shadow on the dial of time, or carry us far into the region of gray antiquity, where history is often merged in the age of fable. But in the fresh life of " Young America," a century reaches to a day of small things in the annals of our ecclesiastical life and civilization. Even our elder sister on the old town plot, (perhaps she may claim a *maternal* relation) will regard us as having just reached the vigorous summer of our existence, her first centennial anniversary having been identical with the date of our ecclesiastical birth.

Had all the incidents and facts of value, connected with the life and progress of our church, been carefully preserved, there would have been a much richer stock of materials, from which to select matter for the present occasion, than our imperfect records afford. For some of these things, which have perished for want of a contemporary historian, I might draw on imagination; but I am aware that a truthful, matter-of-fact narrative is expected. I have, therefore, gleaned from the field of research sundry matters, which, though they may seem barren of interest to those who relish a fresher and more succulent entertainment, have not failed to interest my own feelings. If they fail of meeting a corresponding response on the part of my audience, I must crave their indulgence for the hour, assuring them, that, with such materials as I have been able to collect, I have done the best in my power.

One hundred years ago, and these angular streets, steep declivities, and shady river sides, were occupied by a few plain isolated houses and stores, with little if any of the ornamental appendages and horticultural decorations which we see to-day. Prior to the year 1725, there were no dwelling houses in this part of the town. The land, excepting a few water lots, lay in common with its rugged cliffs, dells and swamps, scattered about in picturesque variety and wildness. It had its romantic attractions and scenery, and its tragic legends of Indian warfare, and was a favorite resort for holiday recreation and rustic sport.

When haying was over in the rural settlements, the young folks were accustomed to muster for a jolly excursion to Norwich Landing, to wander over the hills, climb the rocks, eat oysters, drink flip, and spend the day in fun and frolic.* A

---

* Miss Caulkins' Hist. of Norwich.

daguerreotype of one of those rollicking picnics, with the free and easy manners, and home-spun costume of the brawny swains and buxom maidens, would, I think, possess attractions beyond any of the shows or panoramas of modern exhibition.

At this time Chelsea was little else than " a haven of ships," which sat gracefully on the placid bosom of the Thames, receiving their cargoes from the inland towns, preparatory to a voyage to the West Indies. An impulse had been given to commercial enterprise, the wharves of the Landing presented a busy scene, and the merry shout of the sailor was echoed from these rough hill-sides. Two avenues from the town had been opened on the east and west side of yonder abrupt ridge, which rises between the Yantic and Shetucket, and were connected by Water street, thus forming a winding way round the base of the hill. A ferry plyed between the west bank of the Shetucket and Preston side, and another across the cove to West Chelsea, where some three or four houses had been built.

On pleasant afternoons the ladies of the Landing made equestrian trips up town for the purpose of shopping, that being the emporium of fashion and fancy goods. At the same time they called on their cousins, and cherished the charities of good neighborhood. Perhaps they sent word of their coming ; for in those days of inartificial simplicity, visitors sent notice of their coming, without waiting for any formal invitation, or cards of ceremony.

The generation which then lived and moved amidst these rugged and picturesque localities, was generally of Puritan descent, and possessed those masculine elements of character, and that iron energy, which enabled them to lay strong foundations for a thriving community. Chelsea, with her river privileges, began to look up, and entertain the presumption, that one day she might rival her up-town neighbor. Conscious of their growing importance, and sagacious as to the kind of influences essential to a healthy growth, the people began to consult each other respecting the institutions of religion and education. As yet there was no meeting-house, no church, no preaching. They decided that if they were to compare favorably in point of civilization and morality with the people of the old dominion, they must, like them, inaugurate these institutions. With a view to this end, preliminary measures were taken as early as 1751. Unforeseen embarrassments, and want of union as to plans of operation, delayed the consummation of an object, the importance of which all conceded.

The ecclesiastical Society, with which this church is affiliated, was organized at a meeting held on the 29th day of November, 1751. Captain Dean was chosen Moderator ; Mr. Eleazer Waterman, and Mr. Nathaniel Backus were appointed with him as the committee of the Society for the year. It was voted at the same meeting to erect a sign-post near Mr. Peter Lauman's corner, where notice should be given of future Society meetings. At another meeting, convened on the 10th of December following, it was voted to have preaching four months, and that a tax be laid of one shilling and four pence on the pound, to meet the expenses. Capt. Jabez Dean was appointed to negotiate with Mr. Elijah Lothrop, of Windham, to preach for the Society, and procure a place where to hold meetings.

The next preacher employed, was Mr. John Curtis. At a meeting held April 29th, 1752, it was voted to reward Mr. Curtis by contributions on the Sabbath. Mr. John Elderkin was chosen to treat with him in behalf of the Society. The services of Mr. Curtis were continued a part of the year, till 1754, when a vote to employ him further was passed in the negative. A meeting was called on the 22d of April, 1755, at which it was voted to employ Mr. Ebenezer Cleaveland, to preach one year. There are minutes of other votes on the records of the Society to have preaching, but the names of no other candidates are given. Thus far no steps seem to have been taken to settle a minister in the parish.

On the 30th of June, 1759, it was voted to give Rev. Nathaniel Whitaker, of New Jersey, a call to settle, provided those who were to be organized into a church, should concur and agree as to matters of faith and practice. It was at the same time voted to give Mr. Whitaker one hundred pounds as a settlement, and a salary of one hundred pounds annually, for his support during the time of his ministry.

At a meeting held on the 4th of January, 1760, the following votes were passed : " First, whether the Society do judge it necessary to build a meeting-house for public worship in said Society. Resolved in the affirmative. Second, whether the present Society committee, viz: Jonathan Huntington, Elijah Lothrop and Ephraim Bill, shall be appointed to make application to the County Court for a committee to appoint and afix the place, whereon the said meeting-house shall be erected and built."

In consequence of embarrassments and disagreements, the purpose of building a house of worship was postponed, and not earnestly resumed for several years. Mr. Whitaker accepted the invitation to settle as the minister of the parish, and measures were taken to defray the expense of removing him and his family from New Jersey, where he had been settled. He arrived on the 12th of April, 1760, and immediately directed his efforts to the gathering of a church, before being installed.

The first entry on the records of the church, is in Mr. Whitaker's hand, and as follows : " After many endeavors the church was gathered, and formed by signing a Covenant and Articles of Faith, under the direction of Rev. Messrs. Jabez Wight, and Benjamin Throop, on the 24th day of July, 1760."

The following persons, viz : Nathaniel Whitaker, Nathaniel

Backus, John Porter, Isaiah Tiffany, Nathaniel Shipman and Seth Alden signed the Covenant at the time the church was organized. When the installing council was convened, the following names were added, viz: Jonathan Huntington, William Capron, Caleb Whiting, Jabez Dean, Eleazer Waterman, and Ebenezer Fitch.

As Mr. Whitaker had been connected with a Presbyterian body in New Jersey, he favored that platform of church government. As his agency was prominent in giving form to the church, which he had aided in gathering before his settlement, he had so managed the matter as to secure the adoption of the Presbyterian polity. The plan of church discipline and government, proposed by him, consisted of thirteen articles, which distinctly recognized the authority of a church session consisting of pastor and elders, to which body the entire management of all ecclesiastical business was entrusted. The authority of Presbytery and Synod, as judicatories, was recognized and defined. Among the brethren there was a difference of views in respect to the question of adopting such a platform. It was, however, mutually agreed to submit the matter to the judgment and decision of the council that should be called to install the pastor elect. This council was composed of the following pastors and delegates:

Rev. Benjamin Lord,	Hon. Hezekiah Huntington, delegate.	
" Hezekiah Lord,	Col. Samuel Coit,	"
" Jabez Wight,	Mr. Jabez Fitch,	"
" Eleazer Wheelock,	Mr. Samuel Woodward,	"
" Benj. Throop,	Dea. Simon Lothrop,	"
" Timothy Allen,	Mr. Isaiah Hendy,	"
" Asher Rosseter,	Dea. Jedediah Tracy,	"
" Solomon Williams.		

This council assembled on the 24th of February, 1761, and was organized by the election of Rev. H. Lord, as Moderator, and Rev. Mr. Throop, as Scribe. The first subject that occupied their attention, was the plan of church government, which by agreement was submitted to them. After consultation a result was reached, and recommended for the adoption of the church, before proceeding to the services of the installation. The Cambridge Platform was recommended and accepted as a substitute for the one which had been urged by Mr. Whitaker.* The installation took place on the following day. Rev. Benjamin Lord, pastor of the first church, preached, and his discourse was published.

Some of you may like to be introduced to Mr. Whitaker, whose agency was so prominent in the primary movements of this church. I will present him to your acquaintance, presuming that he is a stranger, of whom most of you have little or no knowledge. He was born in Concord, Mass., and was graduated at Harvard College in the year 1730. His first settlement was in New Jersey, where he acquired such a standing in his profession as to procure from Princeton College the honorary degree of Doctor of Divinity. He was a staunch Presbyterian of the old Scotch stamp, and made an earnest effort to plant that order here. But the two old Puritan Nathaniels, Backus and Shipman, declined coming into such arrangement, and they carried their point, and Congregationalism was the vine here planted.

As a preacher, Mr. Whitaker possessed a high degree of discrimination and force. There was strength, if not beauty, in his ministrations. I infer this from a sermon, preached by him, ninety-eight years ago. It is entitled, "The trial of the Spirits," printed at "Providence, in New England, by Wm. Goddard, near the Court-house." As the printing of a sermon in those days was an event in a man's life, an elaborate preface introduced the discourse, of which the following is an extract: "O! how sad is it, that such multitudes of men and women, youth and children, even where the word of God is powerfully taught, who have Bibles in their hands, and live

---

* See Note A.

2

in Goshen, a land of light, should run headlong in the broad way which leads down to destruction ; * * * * that they should so highly prize and constantly gratify the flesh, which must shortly be food for worms, and so basely slight and neglect their souls ; that every soul-murdering, damning lust should by them be so heartily embraced, and Jesus, the soul-saving Lord, but coldly and complimentally entertained!" In the body of the discourse is found the following : " There is an enthusiastic, anti-christian spirit, which leads poor souls to rest upon impulses, impressions, motions, and what they feel within them, as if they were the ground and reason of their faith and hope ; whereas the true sealing and feeling of the Spirit is the fruit and effect of faith, and not the *ground* of it. ' After ye believed, ye were sealed with the Holy Spirit.' The true Spirit leads the soul to a dependence on Christ without him, even upon Christ in the word of grace and promise, not upon Christ within him, nor upon any created or communicated graces, gifts, experiences, tears, sorrows, joys, forms, feelings, faith, hope, knowledge, or whatever else can be named, that is not God in Christ, exhibited in the word of faith, and covenant of grace."

From such notices, as I have been able to glean from the past, I am confirmed in the conclusion, that he possessed strong elements of character. His style was terse and direct, unpolished, but strong. His executive energy was exhibited in his preliminary movements in this new field. He labored under great disadvantages, arising from want of means, want of harmony between himself and some of the church, and the want of a house of worship. Public worship for several years was maintained in Mr. Samuel Trapp's tavern, Shetucket street, afterwards owned by the late Benjamin Coit, Esq.

From some of the writings of Mr. Whitaker, as well as from traditional statements, it is evident that he was fond of controversy. Some of his people thought that he loved money more than was lawful for a minister, because, finding himself not unfrequently short, he opened a store to eke out his hundred pounds lawful money. He did not go heavily into the grocery business, but limited his traffic to wine, molasses, nutmegs, raisins, salt and pepper, with some other articles in that line. Some of his hearers thought that at times a liberal quantity of the pepper was put into his sermons. He claimed a monopoly of these articles of trade, and if others sold them, he would go in for a spirited competition.

He did not, however, let his merchandize interfere with the discipline of the church. He had its organization completed by the appointment of four ruling Elders ; for his Presbyterian tendencies would now and then creep out in his ecclesiastical measures. I find no record of Deacons. The Elders probably officiated as Deacons, and, perhaps, subsequently took the name. From what may be inferred respecting these men, from the part they took in the affairs of church and society, it is evident that they constituted a strong board of officers. With the pastor, who was rigid in discipline, they aimed to keep things straight in the church. A member is complained of for making too free use of old Jamaica and Santa Croix, articles which the West India commerce introduced into Chelsea market in that day. It was not alleged that he was ever seen drunk, but that he drinked immoderately, and would now and then go on a regular spree. He was accordingly dealt with, as he should have been, and rebuked for such disorderly behavior ; and, persisting in this way of transgression, he was excluded from the church. A young woman, one Sabbath morning, strolled down to the banks of the river after a freshet, to see the ice break up. For this she was called to account, received an official admonition, was subjected to a fine of five shillings, and restored to regular standing. There was one Hannah Forsey, who walked out Sabbath evening with Ede Trapp, upon no religious occasion, which was a scandal, and withal contrary to the statute of the Colony. For this offence she had to appear before the proper authorities, pay three shillings fine, and one shilling cost, and promise that she would not again be so en-*trapped*. There were vigilant Tything-men and grave Elders, whose duty it was to keep the young folks straight, especially on the Lord's day. During the first years of our church, its growth was retarded by various difficulties which those worthy fathers had to encounter. It began with twelve members, and during a period of about eight years only twenty others were added. With great effort the salary of a hundred pounds was raised for the pastor's support. It was not till after many meetings, and much discussion, and protracted effort, that a house of worship, forty-one feet by thirty-seven, was so far completed as to be occupied. This was in the year 1766, nine years after the call for the first meeting at which the proposal for such a building was entertained. It stood on Main street, nearly opposite the house of Mr. William L'Hommedieu. The building was planned for thirty-six pews, which were sold, and the proceeds of sale were applied towards payment for the house.* For a while the bell was suspended on the limb of a tree, as for want of means a steeple was dispensed with. Afterwards a tower was added to the building, in which the bell was hung, and whence its Sabbath chimes rang among these hills and vallies, reminding the good people of the hour of worship. Joseph Smith, a trusty man, was appointed Sexton, to ring the bell and sweep the meeting-house, on a salary of twenty shillings annually, lawful money.

From the time when this religious society was organized, till their house of worship was in a state to be occupied, fifteen years had elapsed—many of them years of discouragement and difficulty. But the few heroic pioneers of this hallowed enterprise persisted in their purpose to plant in this unoccupied field a vine of the right seed. They did not labor

---

* See Note B.

in vain. But though their success was only a day of small
things, it was such as to encourage the hope that the vine
would take strong root, and that under its shadow they would
sit for years to come.

The circumstances in which Mr. Whitaker commenced his
labors, and the misunderstanding which began to exist between him and leading members of the church, made it
manifest that his pastorate would not be a permanent one.
Though a majority of the church adhered to him, he felt that
duty summoned him to some other field of labor, and he proposed to the church that a council be called to take the question of his dismission into consideration, and if they judged
advisable to dissolve the pastoral relation.

Before steps were taken for acting on his request, he was
invited by the " Connecticut Board of Correspondence for
Indian Affairs" to accompany Sampson Occum, the Mohegan
preacher, on a mission to England, to solicit funds for " Moor's
Indian Charity School," then under the care of Dr. Wheelock,
of Lebanon. This novel mission, owing doubtless to the romantic interest created by the presence and appeals of the
first Indian preacher from America who ever visited that
country, proved very successful. Thus the first minister of
this church embarked in a missionary enterprise which had
respect to the conversion of the Pagans of our country. This
event seemed the forthshadowing of a still higher missionary
interest that has become historic. As the result of this primi-
tive mission for our Aboriginal inhabitants, nearly ten thousand pounds sterling were collected, and deposited in the
hands of trustees, subject to the order of Dr. Wheelock, for
the support of his Indian school. Of this sum George III.
gave two hundred pounds, and Lord Dartmouth fifty guineas;
as a compliment to the latter for his generous devotion, his
name was given to Dartmouth College, at the suggestion of
Dr. Wheelock, its first President.

On the return of Mr. Whitaker to Norwich, he did not find things such as to encourage his continuance with his people. Accordingly, at his own request, he was dismissed in March, 1769. On the 28th of July following, he was installed as Pastor of what was then the third church in Salem, Mass. While connected with this church, he aided the society, by his counsels and executive talent, in building a new house of worship in the year 1776, which was dedicated as the "Tabernacle Church"—a name still retained. This church was subsequently occupied by Dr. Worcester, the first Corresponding Secretary of the American Board of Missions. While in Salem, he preached and published a sermon on the death of the celebrated Whitefield. His connection with this church was dissolved in 1783, and in the following year he was settled over a church in what was then the Province of Maine. Continuing there about five years, he was again dismissed, and removed to the State of Virginia, where he died. He published several sermons and pamphlets, which were received at the time as creditable to his head and heart.*

It was more than two years after Mr. W.'s dismission before there was a successful effort to procure a successor. In July, 1771, the church voted unanimously to invite Mr. Ephraim Judson to become their Pastor. The Society convened, and voted an annual salary of one hundred pounds. At the same time a subscription was proposed for the purchase of a parsonage. This effort resulted in raising one hundred and twenty pounds, and the balance of the necessary amount was assured by the Society. Mr. Judson accepted the call, and a council was convened on the 3d of October, 1771, for his ordination. The following pastors and delegates composed the council:

| Rev. Benjamin Lord, | Hezekiah Huntington, delegate. |
| " Jabez Wight, | Daniel Mix, " |

Rev. Asher Rosseter,	Joseph Freeman, delegate.
" Noah Benedict,	Elnathan Judson, "
" Levi Hart,	Elijah Belcher, "
" Aaron Kinne,	Ebenezer Avery, "
" Joel Benedict,	Jacob Perkins, "

The Rev. Noah Benedict preached on the occasion.

A historical sketch of Mr. Judson's life and character may be found in Dr. Sprague's " Annals of the American Pulpit," vol. second. He was born in Woodbury, in the year 1737, and was graduated at Yale College in 1763. His ministry in connection with this church continued about seven years. At his own request, he was released from his pastoral relation in December, 1778. He was subsequently installed as pastor of the Congregational Church in Taunton, Mass., where he remained about ten years. In the year 1791, he was settled in the church at Sheffield, Mass., and retained his pastoral relation thereto till his death, in February, 1813, aged seventy-five. While living in Norwich, he had one child, a son, who was graduated at Williams College, and subsequently studied law. Mr. Judson was an uncle of the distinguished missionary, Adoniram Judson, D. D., who founded the Baptist mission in the Birman empire.

From what I have learned of Mr. Judson, I am led to the conclusion, that he was a man of commanding personal appearance, deliberate in his movements, dignified in his manners, and yet affable to those well acquainted with him. Dr. Chester Dewey, of Rochester, N. Y., whose native place was Sheffield, in a letter to Dr. Sprague, published in his Annals, says: " In his theology he was a decided follower of Dr. Hopkins ; and, being thoroughly acquainted with the system, and withal possessed of a decidedly discriminating mind, and strong logical powers, he would defend his own views with great skill and ability. He had a good knowledge of ecclesiastical history as well as theology, and was altogether a well-read divine of that period. His sermons were marked by great perspicuity and terseness, and abounded in pithy and striking remarks. They contained a large amount of well-digested, well-arranged thought, without any attempt at eloquence of style; and his manner seldom rose to much earnestness."[*]

Eccentricity seems to have been a prominent feature in his character, illustrative of which many amusing anecdotes have come to my knowledge. The late Capt. Erastus Perkins, who died a few years since in the hundred and second year of his age, was one of his early hearers. In a conversation I had with him respecting Mr. Judson, he remarked, that he had the reputation of being both odd and indolent. If he happened to feel weary, he would deliver his sermons in a lounging or sitting posture. In the summer season, when the heat was oppressive, if he wanted a short recess between the prayer and sermon, he would give out a long psalm, such as may be found in Watts' version. For example, he would name, perhaps the 104th Psalm, long metre, beginning at the fourteenth verse:

> "To cragged hills ascends the goat,
> And, at the airy mountain's foot,
> The feebler creatures make their cell;
> He gives them wisdom where to dwell," &c.

While the singing of a dozen verses was going on in the tune, Old Hundred or Hebron, he would retire to a shade in the rear of the church, to catch the breeze which floated up the river; and when singing was ended, he returned to the pulpit, and commenced his sermon.

Miss Caulkins has related some things that illustrate his eccentricity. When preaching on the excuses of the guests, invited to the wedding festival, he remarked with solemn gravity, that they all began to make excuse. The man who had purchased five yoke of oxen, very civilly requested to be ex-

---

cused; but the man who had married a wife, very positively
and hastily declared that he *could not come.* Hence learn,
said the preacher, that one woman can pull more than five
yoke of oxen. What practical application he made of the
inference, does not appear. On some occasion he preached a
sermon to the young women Up-town, in the quaint style of
Hervey's Meditations. He gave it a fictitious and dramatic
form, with a heroine, named *Clarinda.* She was his ideal of
a gay and dashing young woman. He described her fasci-
nating beauty and brilliant wit, introduced her numerous
and rival admirers, recounted her flirtations, dwelt on her
fondness for dress, scenes of gaiety, the amusements of the
ball-room, etc. He traced her course through the flowery
paths of a fashionable, pleasure-seeking life to the sad finale
of the sick chamber, and the bed of death,—weaving into the
discourse fiction and fact, pathos and sentiment. How many
tears were shed over the poor girl's tragic end, is not known;
or how many converts he made among the Town belles of that
day, (for he preached for their special benefit,) no record
informs us. But could he return, clad in the same old
clerical costume, with his venerable white wig to crown his
head, and advertise his lecture on Miss Clarinda, he would,
I think, fill Breed Hall with a curious audience. Possibly
some of his sketches would hit off present times.

During Mr. Judson's ministry but few names are recorded
as having been added to the church. The public mind was
agitated by the political affairs of the colonies, and pending
difficulties with the mother country. The revolutionary con-
flict absorbed the attention, and heavily taxed the resources,
of the people. He sympathised strongly with the popular
spirit of the people, which was earnestly enlisted in the
cause of liberty. Soon after the Declaration of Independence was published, he, yielding to the impulses of a patriotic sentiment, requested and obtained leave of his people to

3

accept a chaplain's commission in Col. Ward's regiment, and was on duty several months, in the service of his country.

Mr. Judson participated warmly with his church and people, and with the colonies, in their self-sacrificing devotion to the cause of civil liberty, then the all-absorbing question of the times. Not satisfied with the degree of influence he could exert in support of this cause within the limits of his parish, he offered his professional services, impatient to share with others in the hardships and perils of the camp, that he might encourage the ill-equipped soldiery by his counsels and prayers—invoking the strength of the Lord of Hosts in support of the noble work, to the achievement of which his people, and the citizens of the town, had so manfully and resolutely pledged themselves. He was in this particular a representative of the patriotic zeal which in that day glowed in the heart of the clergy, and imparted to the ministrations of the pulpit the living power of popular patriotism and heroic resolvings. The growl of Toryism, that clamored about the desecration of the pulpit by political themes, did not intimidate the noble generation of ministers, who then so warmly and heroically espoused the doubtful cause of American freedom.

Rumors of war, the enlistment of soldiers, the furnishing of military stores, and frequent public meetings to discuss the grave questions of the day, so absorbed public attention and feeling, as to create a lamentable state of apathy in respect to the ministrations of the sanctuary. On resuming his parochial work, many discouragements interfered with his professional influence. Suffering from ill health, and crippled in the means of his support, he decided to tender the resignation of his pastorate. Accordingly, he proposed to his people to unite with him in calling a council to dissolve the pastoral relation. His dismission took place December 15, 1778, and he immediately left the place.

[The speaker here paused, remarking, that he would avail himself of a pre-

cedent authorized by his predecessor, Mr. Judson, referred to above, and request the choir to sing a few stanzas, thus affording him a brief recess for
rest. Immediately the following Hymn was sung:]

O God of centuries! draw near,
While glad we crowd thy courts to-day.
For grateful hearts have brought us here,
With joy to trace the gracious way,
In which Thy hand this church has led,
Till now two vines their branches spread.

Here, as thy holy day returns,
Our offering on thine altar burns;
Thy children join in worship high,
Repenting souls for pardon cry,
The meek are bless'd—the proud subdued,
All feel thy presence—gracious God!

One hundred years! swiftly the hours
Have speeded on their censeless flight,
And not one soul is here with ours,
Of those who gathered to unite,
And form this church, a light to be,
To guide earth's wanderers unto Thee!

As a century more rolls by,
And we in dust forgotten lie,
Oh may our happy spirits shine,
In worlds of light and love divine;
And children's children here still raise
To God, our Savior—songs of praise!

The War of the Revolution had now reached a crisis of
intense excitement and painful anxiety. Frequent demands
were made upon the people for money and provisions to sustain the army. While the men bestowed freely such means
as they could command, the women, who had husbands,
brothers and sons in the army, formed associations to make
up garments for the suffering soldiers. All contributed or
labored to sustain the cause, in which all hearts and hands
were united.

From the date of Mr. Judson's dismission, during a period
of nearly nine years, this church remained without a settled
minister. In the meantime, the cause of vital religion suf-

Another of the preachers, employed during this period, was Mr. David Austin, a graduate of Yale College, also one of Dr. Bellamy's theological students. He was a preacher of popular talents, dignified, courteous, eloquent, and impressive. He possessed some marked eccentricities which were amusingly developed in his later years. In preparations for the personal reign of Christ, which he fully believed was at hand, he involved himself in debts which he was unable to cancel. Consequently he was thrown into the debtor's jail in New Haven. Being permitted to have the liberty of the yard, he amused himself sometimes by sporting with a pet horse. One Saturday, he suddenly mounted it and cleared. Two officers were dispatched in pursuit, and overtook him Sabbath afternoon at Lebanon, just as the people had assembled for worship. He hurried into the church, went directly into the pulpit, and insisted on preaching. His pursuers, thinking that they had got him into a corner, quietly took seats below. Immediately he rose, and with an eye to . his pursuers announced his text, John viii, 21: "whither I go ye cannot come." Having closed the service he stepped down from the pulpit, and gracefully surrendered himself.*

Another candidate employed by this society was Mr. Zebulon Ely, a native of Lyme, and graduate of Yale College in 1779. As a company of British soldiers during some part of that year were approaching New Haven, he joined a small company of fellow students, as an advanced post, and kept up a brisk fire upon the enemy. After his comrades had fled, he with heroic spirit maintained his position behind a tree, and continued his fire, till, surprised by a concealed scouting party, who attempted to arrest him, he made good his retreat, amidst a shower of bullets. Mr. Ely studied theology, and was settled in Lebanon. He was the pastor of the senior Governor Trumbull, and preached a

---

* Dr. Sprague's Annals, vol. 2.

fered, the work of conversion ceased, and as very few were added to the church, its strength was seriously impaired. Preaching, however, was statedly supplied, mostly by the employment of young men, candidates for the ministry. Mr. Nathaniel Niles, a graduate of Harvard College, prosecuted his theological studies under the direction of Dr. Bellamy. On applying to the good Doctor to receive him as a student, he was very gravely told that he must give up all his pre-conceived opinions, and begin anew. He did not object to the condition, and received his first theme : " The Existence and Attributes of God," on which he was directed to write. On looking at his subject, he coolly remarked, " I don't believe there is a God." " What," said the astonished Doctor, " come here to study Divinity, and not believe there is a God!" He replied, " I *had* believed there was a God ; but you said, I must give up all my pre-conceived opinions."*

His popular talents procured for him several invitations to settle, but he declined them. He became a resident in Norwich, and officiated in the double capacity of minister and manufacturer. While in this town he wrote that stirring battle ode, " The American Hero," set to a tune prepared for it, and called " Bunker Hill." This became the favorite song in the continental army, which, more than any battle ode of the day, roused the heroism of the soldiers, like the Marseillaise Hymn of the French Revolution.

The spirit of this young man, whose ministrations in this church served to kindle and intensify the fire of patriotism, as well as the life of religion, is exhibited in his stirring verses, of which the following is a specimen. Alluding to the hostile and formidable preparations of the enemy, he says—

> " Fame and dear Freedom *lure* me on to battle,
> While a fell despot, grimmer than a death's head,
> *Stings* me with serpents, fiercer than Medusa's,
> To the encounter."

---

* Sprague's Annals.

Another of the preachers, employed during this period, was Mr. David Austin, a graduate of Yale College, also one of Dr. Bellamy's theological students. He was a preacher of popular talents, dignified, courteous, eloquent, and impressive. He possessed some marked eccentricities which were amusingly developed in his later years. In preparations for the personal reign of Christ, which he fully believed was at hand, he involved himself in debts which he was unable to cancel. Consequently he was thrown into the debtor's jail in New Haven. Being permitted to have the liberty of the yard, he amused himself sometimes by sporting with a pet horse. One Saturday, he suddenly mounted it and cleared. Two officers were dispatched in pursuit, and overtook him Sabbath afternoon at Lebanon, just as the people had assembled for worship. He hurried into the church, went directly into the pulpit, and insisted on preaching. His pursuers, thinking that they had got him into a corner, quietly took seats below. Immediately he rose, and with an eye to . his pursuers announced his text, John viii, 21: "whither I go ye cannot come." Having closed the service he stepped down from the pulpit, and gracefully surrendered himself.[*]

Another candidate employed by this society was Mr. Zebulon Ely, a native of Lyme, and graduate of Yale College in 1779. As a company of British soldiers during some part of that year were approaching New Haven, he joined a small company of fellow students, as an advanced post, and kept up a brisk fire upon the enemy. After his comrades had fled, he with heroic spirit maintained his position behind a tree, and continued his fire, till, surprised by a concealed scouting party, who attempted to arrest him, he made good his retreat, amidst a shower of bullets. Mr. Ely studied theology, and was settled in Lebanon. He was the pastor of the senior Governor Trumbull, and preached a

---

up as a temporary place of worship. Measures were taken to build another meeting-house, and the lot on which this house now stands, was selected as the site of the new building. The money was obtained partly by subscription, and partly by a lottery granted by the General Assembly to raise the sum of £800, which, including liberal donations from Thomas Shaw, Esq., of New London, and Col. Joseph Williams of this city, being their shares of the highest prize in the lottery, encouraged the committee to begin the work.

With the views now entertained of lottery schemes, such a transaction as that just noticed, may seem irregular and objectionable. Our feelings would, at the present day, revolt at the idea of building a house of religious worship by the avails of a lottery. But in former days this mode of raising money for benevolent or patriotic purposes was so conducted as to avoid the offensive features of the system as now managed.

The dimensions of the new house were sixty-two feet in length by forty-two in width. It was substantially built, with a tower surmounted by a tall spire. The services of dedication took place, Dec. 24, 1795, on which occasion a sermon was preached by the Pastor from the text,—"They shall abundantly utter the memory of thy great goodness." It is now sixty-five years since this transaction. From that day this commanding elevation has from Sabbath to Sabbath been visited by religious worshippers, as they have gone up "unto the testimony of Israel, to give thanks unto the name of the Lord." But very few linger among us who can remember the services of that dedication. Pastor and people who rejoiced together on that occasion, have been gathered to their fathers.

From this time the labors of Mr. King were prosecuted harmoniously and prosperously some fifteen years. Additions were made to the church by profession almost every year. In the year 1810, the number of church members was about eighty. The whole number received to the church by profession and letter from the year 1760 to the close of Mr. King's pastoral relation in 1811, was two hundred and thirty-eight.

On the occasion of the death of Washington, he preached a sermon from the text,—" How are the mighty fallen, and the weapons of war perished!" This discourse was characterized by decided ability, pathos, patriotic and christian sentiment. This and his dedication sermon were printed.

Nothing seems to have occurred to disturb the harmony between pastor and people till the year 1810, when a difficulty was suddenly created by differences of opinion in respect to the scripture lawfulness of marriage between a man and the sister of a deceased wife. This unhappy controversy was submitted to a council, convened July 3, 1811, from distant localities, and after protracted deliberation for three days, they voted to dissolve the pastoral relation. In the meantime, they state in their result, that "in the trial of this cause, nothing has been exhibited to impeach his character, (Mr. King,) either as a man, a christian, or a minister of the Gospel." He was accordingly recommended by said council " as an able and faithful minister of the Gospel, in regular and fair standing. The ministers and delegates composing this ecclesiastical council, were the following:

Rev. Joel Benedict, D. D.,
" Elijah Parsons,   Dea. Ephraim Gates, delegate.
" Amos Barrett,   " Sylvester Gilbert,   "
" Azel Backus, D. D.,   David Bellamy,   "
" Calvin Chapin,
" Daniel Dow,   E. Crosby,   "
" Dan Huntington,   Dea. C. Whittlesey,   "
" Lyman Beecher,   Hon. B. Talmadge,   "
" Noah Porter,   Hon. John Treadwell,   "
4

It does not appear that this body of ministers and delegates expressed officially any opinion, as to the lawfulness of such marriage, as in this case constituted the ground of controversy which divided the church, and resulted in the dismission of the pastor. He preached his farewell sermon in August following, founded on the text, "We shall all stand before the judgment seat of Christ." This discourse was published, with an appendix containing a history of the origin and progress of the controversy, and the proceedings of the council, and their result.

Soon after his dismission, Mr. King preached in the city of New York and vicinity about a year. Thence he went to Williamstown, Mass., where, after preaching several months, he received an invitation to settle over the church in that town. His installation took place on the 7th of July, 1813. His work in this field was, however, soon finished. On the first day of December, 1813, he went to the church to deliver a lecture preparatory to the sacramental ordinance. He read a hymn, stood and united in singing, and then prayed with more than usual fervor. He read another hymn, united in singing part of it, and was about to begin his sermon, when, putting his hand to his forehead, he remarked that he should not be able to proceed. He was immediately led from the pulpit and placed in a pew, where he was heard to say he was cold. These were his last words. He was carried to his house, and died the same day of an appoplectic fit. President Moore, of Williams College, preached on occasion of his funeral, from the text, "My times are in thy hand."*

In the autumn of 1811, the Rev. Asahel Hooker, who had been settled in Goshen, Litchfield county, was invited to preach in this parish. Mr. Hooker was a lineal descendant from the distinguished Puritan minister, Rev. Thomas Hooker, the first pastor of the church in Hartford. In consequence of

* Panoplist, vol. 12.

ill health, he had tendered his resignation of his pastoral charge. He was enabled, however, to renew preaching after a season of rest, and for a time preached in New Haven, and in the Spring-street Presbyterian Church in New York.

It was a kind providence that called him to this church, at a time when the division, created among the people by Mr. King's dismission, was yet unhealed. He was pre-eminently a common sense, conciliatory man, a peace-maker, a "judicious Hooker," whose timely counsels, benign spirit, and acceptable ministrations, gradually allayed the elements of bitterness, and restored harmony. He received a call to the pastorate of the church, which he accepted. His installation took place in January, 1812, on which occasion Dr. Nott, of Franklin, preached. He entered on his labors with an earnest spirit, and the promise of distinguished usefulness. His preaching was direct and pungent. In theology, he was of the Edward-ean school, and was regarded as a sound and thorough doctrinal preacher. He had aided many young men in their studies preparatory to the ministry, by whom he was remembered and beloved.

Sometime in April, 1813, he was seized with a fever, then prevalent in the place, and in a few days died, in the fifty-first year of his age. He met the sudden summons with a submissive, triumphant spirit. His people were deeply affected by the bereavement experienced in the sudden removal of their pastor, whom they loved and respected as "a man full of faith and of the Holy Ghost." Dr. Humphrey, formerly President of Amherst College, was one of Mr. Hooker's theological pupils. In a letter to Dr. Sprague, he speaks of him as follows: "He was a man of remarkable mildness and equanimity of temper. His face was the mirror of a lovely disposition. His smile attracted you like the opening of a spring morning. On his tongue was the law of kindness, and he entered so warmly into all your interests, that you could not help giving him your entire confidence. * * * * He was a good man, of excellent talents and high professional acquirements; a devoted pastor; an edifying and searching preacher; a wise counsellor; an earnest defender of the faith once delivered to the saints."*

Mr. Hooker left a wife and three children to mourn the loss of a devoted husband, and affectionate father. His widow was subsequently married to Samuel Farrer, Esq., of Andover, Mass. His son, Rev. Edward Hooker, D. D., late Professor in the East Windsor Theological Institute, and his two daughters, Mrs. Cornelius and Mrs. Peck, are yet living. His grave is with us in the old cemetery, marked by a plain monument.

The commencement of Mr. Hooker's ministry in this city was identified with the organization of the Foreign Missionary Society of Norwich and vicinity. A circular, containing a well written appeal on the subject of Foreign Missions, then just beginning to enlist public sympathy and patronage, together with a constitution, was issued and sent to pastors and churches in the vicinity.† This society, a few years since, was united with that of New London and vicinity, and embraces the whole county as its field. Its next annual meeting will be the forty-ninth, being but one year younger than the American Board, which will celebrate its Jubilee in October.

At a meeting of this church, held April 25th, 1814, measures were adopted to extend an invitation to Mr. Alfred Mitchell to become its Pastor. Mr. M. was the youngest son of Hon. Stephen M. Mitchell, Wethersfield, Chief Justice of the State. He was graduated at Yale College in 1809, commenced theological studies with Rev. Dr. Porter, then pastor of the church in Washington, and accompanied him to the Theological Seminary, Andover, Mass., on his appointment as a Professor in that Institution. He there com-

---

* Sprague's Annals, vol. 2.　　　　　† See Note E.

29

pleted a regular course of study. The society concurred
with the church in its vote to call Mr. Mitchell, and offered
him a yearly salary of seven hundred dollars. In a charac-
teristic letter* he accepted the invitation, and was ordained
October, 1814.

The ecclesiastical council convened to ordain Mr. Mitchell consisted of the following pastors and delegates:

Rev. Samuel Nott, D. D.	Ashbel Woodward, delegate.
" Levi Nelson,	Freeman Tracy, "
	Dea. Elias Perkins, "
" Nathaniel W. Taylor, D. D.,	
" Cornelius B. Everest,	Dea. Wm. Cleveland, "
" Joel Hawes, D. D.,	Lewis Weld, "
" Charles Hyde,	Wm. C. Gilman, "
" Edward Bull,	Hubbard Dutton, "
" Seth Bliss,	Nath'l Coit, "
" Barnabas Phinney,	Dea. Ebenezer Allen, "
" Geo. J. Tillotson,	Dea. Edwin Newbury, "

The Rev. Prof. Porter of Andover preached on the occasion.

The people gathered around their young minister with
confidence and co-operation, and heartily engaged in efforts
to promote the peace and prosperity of the church. His labors were prosecuted diligently, studiously, and with singular
discretion. Signs of promise now cheered and encouraged
his heart. A large addition was made to the church by profession during the years 1820 and 1821. And in the meantime there was an increasing attendance on the services
of the sanctuary.

The growth of the congregation required an enlargement
of the house of worship. The addition and the remodeling
of the interior were completed in the year 1829. Mr. Mitch-

* See Church Records, Vol. 1, p. 76.

ell was very active in urging forward this improvement, and though his salary was only seven hundred dollars, he contributed one-fourth of it that year to aid in these improvements. Some who were active members of the society at that time, have expressed the regret that they allowed him to bear so disproportionate a share of the expense incurred by the society.

On the return of the congregation to the house, the pastor preached an excellent discourse, appropriate to the occasion, from the text, " The glory of this latter house shall be greater than the former." This discourse was printed. From the spirit manifested in this sermon, it is evident that he was anticipating a speedy realization of the import of his text, passages from which, did my limits permit, I would gladly introduce, as showing the heart of the man, as well as his power. It was not long before his earnest aspirations and hopes were followed with " times of refreshing," marked with unusual power, the fruits of which were choice and abundant. During the year 1830, as our catalogue shows, eighty-nine were added to the church by profession, and in the year following sixty others, making in all one hundred and forty-nine. Many of this number were heads of families. Seldom has a revival of religion resulted in so great an accession of strength, maturity, talent, and executive influence to a church. As might have been expected from the known character of the pastor, he experienced and expressed intense solicitude, that all who had thus come out publicly on the Lord's side, might adorn their profession by steadfastness and consistency. He took occasion to prepare a discourse, specially adapted to the case of persons who were young in religious experience. It was an affectionate and faithful pastoral message of counsel, exhortation, and encouragement. The text of this discourse was from 1 Thessalonians, 3 : 8. "For now we live, if ye stand fast in the Lord." It

was published, and whoever reads it, will feel that it was
worthy of the man and of the occasion.

With a renovated house of worship, and a revived, active,
united church, the Pastor, then in noon of active manhood,
must have anticipated many years of happy intercourse and
prosperous labor among his attached people. But God had
otherwise ordered. Towards the close of the year 1831, he
was attacked by disease which resulted in death on the 19th
of December, in the forty-second year of his age. His amia-
ble and excellent wife, the oldest son, and two daughters,
have since followed him, and their graves are with us.

The most favorable testimonials to the character and min-
isterial qualifications of Mr. Mitchell have been furnished,
not only by his published discourses, but by surviving members of the church, then under his pastoral care. The Rev.
Albert T. Chester, D. D., of Buffalo, N. Y., who in early
years enjoyed the pastoral instructions of Mr. Mitchell, remarks in a letter, published in Sprague's Annals,* as follows:
" His sermons were always most carefully studied and written. It was well understood that he would not preach to his
people, unless his sermon had been finished to please him,
but would exchange with some neighboring pastor, and take
another week to make his work complete. * * * * Nor
were his discourses merely correct in style and unobjectiona-
ble in expression,—polished but pointless: they often contained passages of great power, which, delivered as they were
with increased animation, fairly startled the congregation."
Mrs. Sigourney of Hartford, in a letter published in the same
connection, has given a beautiful tribute to his character as a
man and a christian minister. Referring to him as being
averse to theological controversy and metaphysical hair split-
ting, or a severe supervision of differing opinions, she
says:

" Not of that band was he who toil and strive,
To pluck the mote out of their brother's creed,
Till charity's forgotten plant doth miss
The water-drop and die ; but of the few
Who bear Christ's precept on their lip and life,—
See that ye love each other."

In addition to the two discourses already noticed, Mr. Mitchell published a sermon on the death of Mrs. Sarah Lanman, another on the death of Bela Peck Williams, a youthful son of Gen. William Williams, and one prepared for the " Saybrook Platform " meeting.

On the fourth of April, 1832, Rev. James Taylor Dickinson, a graduate of Yale College and of the Theological Institution therewith connected, was ordained as pastor of this church. Dr. Taylor, of New Haven, preached on the occasion. He entered upon his work under very favorable circumstances, and with an earnestness of spirit and honesty of purpose that won the confidence and efficient co-operation of a strong church, that had just been vitalized by power from on high. At the time of his settlement there was more than usual religious sensibility, which favored his work. During the first year of his ministry, thirty-three persons were added to the church by profession. In the early part of the year 1834, a protracted meeting was held, and continued several successive days. A very general religious interest was created through the society and community, and a large number expressed the hope of conversion. As the result of this awakening, eighty-five were united to the church. The number received on profession, during Mr. D.'s brief ministry, was one hundred and seventy-one. At this time the number of the church members resident in the place was about three hundred and twenty-five. The number of families, that considered themselves as belonging to the society, was one hundred and thirty ; embracing a few over six hundred persons.

Having continued his labors about two and a half years, Mr. Dickinson, yielding to the conviction that duty called him to labor in the field of Foreign Missions, resigned his pastorate, and his relation to the church was dissolved, Aug. 20, 1834. After devoting himself several months to preparatory studies with special reference to the missionary work, he took his departure for his distant field among the heathen. In the early part of the year 1836, he reached the island of Singapore, to which station he had been appointed. Events operating unfavorably in respect to this mission, it was given up by the Board, and not long after, Mr. D. resigned his connection therewith and returned.

This church is affiliated to others of recent organization, to which some of its members were transferred by letters of dismission and recommendation. The first was that organized at Norwich Falls, Aug. 29, 1827. This church had a prosperous, though brief history. Its last meeting was on the 23d of May, 1842, when some of its leading members united with what is now the Broadway Church. As early as 1816, a Sabbath School was established at the Falls, and formed the nucleus of the church, which, at the time of its organization, consisted of only ten members, some of whom were from our church. Several seasons of religious revival were enjoyed, by which it was enlarged and promised permanency. The first minister was Rev. Benson C. Baldwin, installed, June 31, 1828, and dismissed, Aug. 18, 1829. The next was Rev. Charles Hyde, installed, Jan. 2, 1830, and dismissed, Oct. 4, 1834. The third was Rev. Joel W. Newton, installed, Oct. 29, 1834, and dismissed, Jan. 4, 1837. The last, Rev. Thomas K. Fessenden, was ordained, Oct. 16, 1839, and dismissed, Feb. 17, 1841. Up to this last date, one hundred and fifty-seven had been added to the church, of whom ninety were received on profession. Changes in the business of that village, and the establishment of the Broadway Church, led

5

to the dissolution of this, and the clerk was authorized to give to the members letters of recommendation to other churches.

The Congregational Church at Greeneville was organized, Jan. 1, 1833, and was composed of sixteen members, of whom six were from this church. The first Pastor, Rev. John Storrs, was installed, March 12, 1834, and dismissed, April 17, 1835. The Rev. Stephen Crosby commenced his labors in the society in the fall of 1836, received and accepted a call to settle, but his installation was for some reason deferred, though he continued his labors, until his decease in June, 1838. The Rev. A. L. Whitman was installed, Dec., 1838, and dismissed, March, 1846. Rev. Charles P. Bush was installed Dec., 1846, and dismissed in June, 1856. Rev. Robert P. Stanton was installed, June, 11, 1856. There have been received to this church to June, 1860, four hundred and fifty members. The present number is 209.

On the 24th of May, 1842, seventy-eight members of our church were dismissed for the purpose of being organized with others into the Fifth, now Broadway Church. Most of these persons were then in the vigor and strength of their years, and by their removal an important portion of the entire membership of the church was taken away. The change for a reason, though the necessity for it was felt and acknowledged, exerted a somewhat depressing influence upon those who remained. The number of resident members, after the division, was two hundred and twenty-seven, among whom were the aged and infirm, who did not feel like engaging in a new enterprise. This church was organized June 1, 1842. The congregation occupied the Town Hall, as their place of worship, till Oct. 1845, when their house, erected on Main street, was dedicated. In Aug. 1842, Rev. Willard Child was installed Pastor, and continued till Aug. 1845, when his resignation was accepted. The present Pastor, Rev.

J. P. Gulliver, was ordained, and installed over the church, Oct. 1, 1846. It has shared, in common with our own church, in several powerful revivals of religion. The number of members has steadily increased, till it now numbers about three hundred and forty, a larger number than belonged to our church, before the separation took place.

The house of worship, first erected by this society on Main street, was burnt down, and the one now occupied, was dedicated, Oct. 13, 1857.

The history of our ecclesiastical affairs during the period of twenty-five years, the time of the present pastorate, is so well known, that it will not be of special interest to dwell upon it, even were there time for a detailed account. The first Sabbath in May last, closed the twenty-fifth year of the present Pastor's labors in this field.*

These twenty-five years, in passing away, have witnessed many and marked changes in our church and congregation. On reviewing the records of this church, as they were when I entered this field of labor, I find only about fifty then on the register, now enrolled among our resident members. There have been one hundred and eighty-six removals by death. Of this number fifty-six reached a good old age, having passed the limit of three score years and ten, one-half of them lived, till over eighty, and one over a hundred years. While removals have been taking place by death and dismission, additions have been made, and the vacant places have been occupied by others. During the present pastorate, five hundred and fifty have been received to this church. The ordinance of infant baptism has been administered to two hundred and forty-four children, some of whom have since professed their faith in Christ.

In the spring of 1844, our house of worship was so injured by fire, that it was decided to have it taken down, and to re-

---

* See Note F.

build of stone on the same site. This edifice was dedicated
to the worship of God on the 1st of January, 1846. The sermon on the occasion was founded on the text, Psalms, 96 : 6,
" Strength and beauty are in thy Sanctuary," and was published.*

This church and society have not only made generous pro-
vision for the support of the ministrations of the Gospel at
home, but have freely responded to the numerous and re-
peated calls of christian benevolence, as they have been presented. For several years past not less than thirty-six hundred dollars annually have been raised for the maintenance
of public worship. The contributions to objects of benevolence have varied in amount in different years, rising in some
years to a high figure, in consequence of special appeals.
During the last year these contributions have not been less
than four thousand dollars.

From a historical sketch of the Sabbath School, prepared
by the present Superintendent, (Dea. George Coit,) it appears that in the summer of 1815, a few colored boys were
collected in a house on Franklin street. From the first report of the teachers it appears, that they commenced with
five scholars, which increased to forty-one, some of whom
were adults. The persons who engaged in this Sabbath mission labor were, Charles S. F. Harrington, Asa Roath, and
D. T. Hinckley. In 1816, another school for white boys was
established in the school house, which stood near where the
Town Hall now stands. The colored school was united with
this, and the whole number registered after the union, was
forty-eight. Reading was taught as one of the school exercises. In the summer of the same year, a school for girls
was collected by a few young ladies, none of whom at the
time were professors of religion. It met in the porch of the
meeting house, and there continued till the weather became

* See Note G.

cold, when it was removed to the house where the other
school assembled, each school occupying separate rooms. The
number of girls was forty-seven, between the ages of four
and twelve. Miss C. M. Marvin was the Superintendent.

In the year 1818, these schools were united under one
Superintendent, Mr. Wm. C. Gilman. He commenced a
record of the school, which has been continued to the present
time. In 1820, it contained one hundred and fifty-one scholars and twenty-four teachers. To encourage this enterprise,
there was organized in Oct. 1816, the "Chelsea Sunday
School Union Society," which had quarterly meetings, at
which the progress of the school was reported. The succes-
sors of Mr. Gilman, as Superintendents, were Horace Colton,
J. G. W. Trumbull, and Charles Coit. The primary aim of
those who engaged in this enterprise, was limited to the children of families that did not attend public worship. It was
a home mission movement. Soon however, the field was enlarged, and the children of the congregation were numbered
in the Sabbath School. From the beginning, it was resolved
to continue the school through the year. From that day to
the present, a period of forty-four years, it has been assembled as regularly as the worshipping congregation.

A missionary association has been organized in the school,
and a monthly contribution has been received. The amount
contributed last year was a little above ($166) one hundred
and sixty-six dollars. From the avails of this fund a Sunday
School missionary is supported. A Home mission enterprise
has recently been undertaken, and a school house built by the
liberal donations of friends of the cause. The number on
our Sabbath School register at the present time, is somewhat
more than three hundred and fifty, besides fifty or sixty connected with the Branch School. The largest attendance during the past year was three hundred and forty-seven, and the
average attendance has been two hundred and eighty-nine.

On reviewing the records of our school, the names of seventeen are found, who have become ministers of the Gospel. Four others have died while preparing for the ministry.* There has been an onward progress in the prosperity of this cherished institution, from its very small beginning to the present time.

The institutions of christian benevolence have received from this church cheerful and steady patronage. The cause of Foreign Missions, more than any other, has enlisted its sympathies, and received essential aid, not only in pecuniary contributions, but in the personal labors and sacrifices of its members. No sooner was the American Board of Foreign Missions organized, than its claims were responded to by our church, which has never failed of forwarding annually its free-will offerings to sustain this noble society. The proximity of the Mohegan neighborhood of aboriginal inhabitants, early suggested the idea of missionary labor for the conversion of the unevangelized. The mission of Dr. Whitaker and Sampson Occum was a preliminary measure in the missionary enterprise, inaugurated ninety-four years ago. This church, in its early infancy, was thus baptized into the missionary spirit, and during the last half century it has steadily shared in the honor and privilege of sending the Gospel to the Gentiles.

Occum, the Mohegan convert, was the first missionary, to whose encouragement this church contributed. He labored at first among the Montauk Indians on the east end of Long Island, and subsequently went on a mission to the Oneida Indians, where he labored with success. It is worthy of remark, that our first missionary to the pagans was a man who was born a pagan, and who after his conversion and education, aided by the Pastor of this church, became a pioneer in the missionary work. But the spirit of missions, thus

* See Note H.

early developed, in connection with the now wasted tribe of Mohegans, received a check from the operation of various causes, particularly the disturbing excitement and absorbing influence of the war of Independence ; and except in domestic operations it was not again awakened, till kindled in the hearts of those young men, Mills, Judson, Hall, and Nott, who breathed their spirit into the soul of the General Association of Massachusetts forty-four years afterwards. This church at once sympathized in this revival of the missionary life, and from that day has been ready to part with her sons and daughters, and pecuniary contributions to help forward the work of the world's conversion. Norwich, including its original limits, has furnished for the work of missions to the heathen, thirty missionaries.* Some of these have gone from our own church. Among the number will be recognized the cherished name of Sarah Lanman Smith. Her heroic devotion to the missionary work was early manifested in the laborious and self-denying services she rendered, in elevating the depressed and neglected remnant of the ever friendly tribe of Mohegans to a state of christian civilization. Seeing them fast sinking beneath the pressure of neglect, and scorn, and moral degradation, lying by the wayside, sick and wounded, with none to care for their souls, she as an angel of kindness undertook the almost hopeless task of raising them to the plane of christianized humanity, and inspiring them with hope and self-respect. In summer heat and wintry cold her weekly pilgrimage was made to this weak and scattered people. And by her persevering efforts she planted among them the school house and the church, and left on their hearts the ineffaceable impress of her noble example of self-denying devotion to their temporal and spiritual welfare. The fragrance of her memory will be preserved there, till the last of the Mohegans has disappeared from earth. Thence

* See Note I.

she went far hence to the heathen, to teach the wild children in the mountains of Lebanon the Gospel of Jesus. And there she labored on till the Master called her home.

In 1842, the American Board of Foreign Missions met in this place. The known interest which the people of Norwich had manifested in the cause of Missions, called together a very large meeting, much larger than had ever before been convened. There were present sixty-three corporate members, two hundred and ninety-two honorary members, eight returned missionaries, and Mar Yohannan, the Nestorian Bishop; in all three hundred and sixty-four, besides a much larger number of friends of the missionary cause. The meeting was one of unprecedented interest, and gave a new impulse to the missionary spirit in our churches. All felt that it was good to be present, and share in the soul-stirring and elevating services of the occasion. The committee of arrangements was composed, besides myself, of Rev. H. P. Arms, Charles W. Rockwell, William C. Gilman, and F. A. Perkins.

From this church and society there have gone forth many persons, who have been lights and pillars in church and state. A catalogue of the sons and residents of Norwich, who have received degrees from colleges, may be found in the appendix of Mr. Gilman's Bi-Centennial Discourse. The total number of graduates from Norwich, as it was, is two hundred and forty-two. Of this number all but nineteen have been graduated during the last hundred years, of whom many have been connected with families belonging to this church and society.

This church has proved a favorable school for the training of a goodly number of worthy Deacons, by whom she has been well served, and is so still. In 1763, there were chosen as *Elders*, Messrs. Jabez Dean, Nathaniel Shipman, Isaiah Tiffany, and Jonathan Huntington. As there were only eleven male members of the church at this time, exclusive of the pastor, I think, that with four such men, invested with the double office of elders and deacons, it was, as we have noticed, pretty thoroughly governed. Elder Shipman was a Congregationalist of the straitest sect, and, jealous of Mr. Whitaker's Presbyterian proclivities, he protested against his platform, and being a firm old Puritan in principle, he ruled out the elements that conflicted with pure Congregationalism, giving preference to the old Cambridge Platform, which was at last adopted. Reliable tradition, in the absence of official record, assures us that Jonathan Lawrence, Jonathan Huntington, and John Corning officiated as deacons, and then we have on record the names of Samuel Rudd, Jabez Huntington, William Rogers, Francis A. Perkins, Horace Colton, Hamlin B. Buckingham, Charles Coit, Joseph Otis, George Perkins, William Williams, George Coit, and Claudius B. Webster.

Deacons sometimes, perhaps not without some cause, have acquired the reputation of Diotrephes, who made himself notorious in one of the apostolic churches. But it gives me pleasure to state, that I have not found, either from historical or personal knowledge, any disposition manifested by the officers of this church to assume responsibilities that did not legitimately pertain to their official work.

There have gone forth from this church men who have acquitted themselves with honor in the responsible positions of civil and political trust, to which they have been promoted. Some have with ability occupied the judicial bench in our higher courts of justice. Others have represented the State with honor in both houses of Congress. And the citizen, who at the present time occupies the executive chair of our Commonwealth with distinguished ability, was formerly a member of this church. Her members and her children may be found in every part of our land, from the forests of

6

Maine to the placers of California, and from the remotest points of the sunny South, to the snows of Canada. And in many instances it has been, and still is known, that in their wide-spread emigrations they have carried with them their Puritan integrity and religious principles, and maintained them.

This leads me to remark, that there was originally incorporated into this church and society a large mixture of the Puritan and Saxon stock. The leading men were lineal descendants of the earliest settlers of New England. This fact I learn from an inspection of the names, found on our early records, and in tracing their genealogy. They were genuine off-shoots of charter-oak nobility, possessing its early vigor, as when it held in its bosom the *magna charta* of our freedom, but none of its elements of decay. They live in their offspring and in their deeds, and though that time-honored tree has bowed its venerable head before the storm-blast, the sturdy founders of this church and society live in the superstructure of which they laid the foundations—live in the sons and daughters who succeed them.

Among the names on the records of this church and society, the following are found: Arnold, Barstow, Breed, Bill, Bushnell, Backus, Bliss, Clement, Carew, Coit, Dean, Dennis, DeWitt, Edgerton, Elderkin, Fitch, Huntington, Hubbard, Howland, Lamb, Leffingwell, Lanman, Lester, Lothrop, Kingsbury, Miner, McCurdy, Perkins, Peabody, Rockwell, Roath, Smith, Trumbull, Tiffany, Tracy, Trapp, Warren, Wetmore, Wight, Whiting, and some others. Of the Huntingtons, four are named as having been active in the affairs of the society in the early period of its existence. The chairman of the society committee in 1752 was Benedict Arnold, father of the traitor,—whose mother is represented as "a patern of patience, piety, and virtue." A letter, which she wrote to her son Benedict when at school in another town, furnishes evidence of her exemplary maternal qualities. In this letter she says to him, "keep a steady watch over your thoughts, words, and actions. Be dutiful to superiors, obliging to equals, and affable to inferiors"—advice which seems to have been dictated by the knowledge she possessed of his restless, passionate, and reckless disposition, so lamentably developed in his subsequent career of profligacy, treachery, and revenge.

In the retrospect we have taken of our ecclesiastical history for the hundred years this day completed, much has been necessarily omitted. The limits of a single discourse will allow nothing more than a rapid notice of the men who have been the prominent actors, and the affairs included in its history. Enough however has been said to awaken sentiments of gratitude to the Head of the Church in view of the past, and of trust for the future.

This vine was trained amidst "troublous times." From the year 1760 to 1790 the country was involved in civil and political agitations, in an exhaustive war, with its impoverishing and demoralizing influences, and in sharp internal conflicts, before the foundations of the government were settled. It was a transition age, in the affairs of which a generation expended a heavy amount of time, treasure and blood. After the darkest clouds of that stormy period had passed by, there appeared many portentous signs in the political skies, that threatened disaster to the ark of freedom, which had just been launched on a sea of anxious experiment.

It is not strange, that in such circumstances this vine, then young, should have been retarded in its growth and development. During the period of fifty years, only two hundred and fourteen were added to the original number of six, when organized. During the last fifty years the additions have amounted to one thousand and thirty-six, of which number more than half have been added during the present pastorate.

Most devoutly should we recognize the good hand of our God in his dealings with this our beloved church, whose early foundations were laid amidst the struggles of self-denial, with many prayers and tears. When the storms of adversity beat upon her in her weakness, though shaken, and sometimes cast down, she was not destroyed. The elements of Puritan soundness, firmness, intelligence, integrity and faith, incorporated in her membership and ministry, acted as a conservative agency, and, under God, she was enabled to endure and grow, slowly indeed for a season, but sure and symmetrical.

This has been a well watered garden. Times of refreshing have often visited it, and caused it to bud and blossom, and bring forth large and precious harvests. In many of these seasons, we, who are among the living, have shared and rejoiced. And many who have here finished their course, have been garnered to their resting place in the better land. How many hundreds who worshipped in connection with this church, have passed away! Pastors and people are this have met in another world. For this dear church they labored and prayed, and, having been called home, the precious trust is committed unto us, to care for, and pray for, and live for, till we too shall be summoned to follow them.

Could the early members of this church have been able to look down the long vista of a hundred years, and witnessed what we see to-day, how would their hearts have swelled with holy joy and exultation! Could we look through the intervening distance, and have a glimpse of the next centennial, we, doubtless, should behold a jubilee in which there would be commemorated still nobler triumphs, and the record of richer displays of a Savior's love and grace than the past has witnessed. That day of jubilee will come; but none of us will be there to participate in its gratulations and services. Where shall we then be? Serious, solemn inquiry! O may our course be such, that when it is finished, we on that day shall be rejoicing in a more glorious jubilee in our Father's house.

APPENDIX.

At a meeting of the Second Congregational Church held April 24, 1860, the following votes were passed :—

Resolved, That this Church (Providence permitting) will observe the hundredth anniversary of its organization on the 24th of July next.

Resolved, That brothers WILLIAM WILLIAMS, JOHN A. ROCKWELL, EBENEZER LEARNED, CHARLES JOHNSON, SAMUEL H. GROSVENOR, FRANCIS A. DORRANCE, C. B. WEBSTER, DAVID SMITH, and GEORGE PERKINS be appointed a Committee to cause the foregoing resolution to be carried into effect.

S. B. MEECH, Clerk pro tem.

At a meeting of the Committee, appointed by the foregoing resolution, held May 4th, Deacon WM. WILLIAMS was appointed Chairman, and FRANCIS A. DORRANCE, Clerk.

Resolved, That it is expedient, in celebrating the Centennial Anniversary of the organization of this church, that an appropriate historical discourse should be delivered at the church in the forenoon, accompanied by suitable religious services ; and that in the afternoon a collation be provided, with music and speeches, at some suitable place in the open air, or, if the weather should be unfavorable, in Breed Hall, or some other public place.

Resolved, That all the members of the congregation be requested to co-operate in this celebration ; and that the Sabbath School, under the charge of the Superintendent and Teachers, be invited to participate in the religious and festive services of the day.

WM. WILLIAMS, D. SMITH, and E. LEARNED were appointed a Committee to invite Rev. Dr. BOND to deliver the Historical Discourse, and to make arrangements for the exercises in the forenoon.

G. PERKINS, C. B. WEBSTER, S. H. GROSVENOR were appointed a Committee to make arrangements for the afternoon exercises.

48

C. Johnson and F. A. Dorrance were appointed a Financial Committee.

J. A. Rockwell and E. Learned were appointed a Committee to invite absent or former members of the church.

F. A. DORRANCE, *Clerk of Com.*

The following circular was sent by the Committee :

CHURCH CENTENNIAL.

The Second Congregational Church, of Norwich, has decided to celebrate the Centennial Anniversary of its organization, and to carry this purpose into effect, has appointed a Committee, consisting of Messrs. Wm. Williams, David Smith, George Perkins, Charles Johnson, Claudius B. Webster, Samuel H. Grosvenor, Francis A. Dorrance, John A. Rockwell, and Ebenezer Learned.

In making the arrangements for this Celebration, the committee have entrusted to the undersigned the duty of inviting the former members of the church to unite with us, on the 24th day of July next, in the endeavor to show our gratitude "for mercies past received," and in supplication for a continuance of gracious blessings on the church which has been so long a watered vine of God's own planting.

It is arranged that an Historical Address be delivered by Rev. Dr. Bond, the Pastor, in the morning, with appropriate religious services, at the church; and in the afternoon, that there be a Social Gathering of the Church and Congregation, together with the Sabbath School.

All persons who have been at any time members of the church, and are now attached to other churches, whether in Norwich or elsewhere, are respectfully invited to be present.

You are earnestly requested to unite with us on this occasion.

Very truly,

JOHN A. ROCKWELL, } *Committee.*
EBENEZER LEARNED, }

Norwich, May 17th, 1860.

On Tuesday, July 24, at 10 o'clock, A. M., public services were conducted in the church in accordance with the following order of exercises :

1. A Voluntary was performed by the choir.
   "Songs of praise the angels sung," &c.
2. A selection of Scriptures was read by Rev. Thomas L. Shipman, of Jewett City.
3. Prayer was offered by Rev. H. P. Arms, Pastor of the First Church.
4. An Original Hymn, by Anson G. Chester, of Buffalo, N. Y., was sung.

Tune— Ward.

A century's suns have shone and set,
  Since first our pious fathers met,
And builded here a holy shrine,
  And planted here a tender vine.

Through all the long and weary years,
  That vine they watered with their tears;
God saw their vigils, heard their cries,
  And sent a blessing from the skies.

That shrine by many a foot was sought;
  That vine a glorious fruitage brought;
Jehovah bade the blossoms start,
  And twined the tendrils 'round His heart.

Oh God! thy gracious ear incline,
  To those who keep this larger vine;
And give it rain and dew and sun,
  And take its clusters for thine own.

And when our watchful eyes shall close,
  And death shall bring us sweet repose,
Still let this vine receive thy care—
  Still let it thrive and let it bear!

Oh may this shrine be made thy home,
  Through all the changing years to come;
And, tears and toils and struggles past,
  Fathers and children meet at last!

5. A Historical Discourse was delivered by the Pastor of the Church.

6. An Original Hymn, by Miss F. M. CAULKINS, was sung.

Tune—Majesty.

We praise thee, Lord, that thou did'st found,
  This church on Christ, the Rock;
And still hast kept it walled around,
  From error's fatal shock.

Praise for the souls of priceless worth,
  Renewed and nurtured here;
Praise for our vine's celestial birth,
  And for our hundredth year.

7

Praise for the pure and honored names,
Upon our shield enrolled ;
For *Niles,* [1] whose fame the nation claims,
For *King,* [2] devout and bold.

For *Hooker,* [3] 'mid the angels sphered,
For *Mitchell,* [4] crowned and blest :
For *living guides,* [5] whose light has cheered,
Full many a darkened breast.

For trials that the church refine,
For good men passed away :
For yon fair scion from our vine,[6]
Our sister church to-day.

Now, Savior, let thy grace divine,
Fall on us like the dew ;
Say to thy church, Arise and shine !
Revive our love anew.

So may the century we begin,
High o'er the past ascend ;
A nobler throng of converts win—
In loftier anthems end.

F. M. C.

An invitation was then given to the Congregation and the Sabbath School, to meet in a social gathering at the grove in the rear of the " Free Academy," at 3 o'clock in the afternoon.

The exercises of the Anniversary were resumed by a numerous social gathering in the afternoon in the grove according to the preceding notice. The Sabbath School was formed in procession at the church, and, preceded by a band of music, marched to the ground, where preparations had been made for their reception and entertainment. The number was large, and their appearance, and good order elicited the expression of general satisfaction. Members of the church and congregation, and many who were formerly connected

1. Rev. Nathaniel Niles, the patriot preacher of the Revolution, author of the beautiful ode, entitled, " The American Hero."
2. Rev. Walter King, ordained May 21, 1787.
3. Rev. Asahel Hooker, installed Jan. 16, 1812.
4. Rev. Alfred Mitchell, ordained Oct. 27, 1814.
5. Rev. James T. Dickinson, dismissed in 1834, to go on a mission to China, and Rev. Alvan Bond, D. D., the present pastor.
6. The Broadway Congregational Church,—a colony from the Second Church, organized June 1, 1842.

therewith, were assembled in large numbers to participate in the services and festivities of the occasion. The grove of native forest trees was attractive, and the weather sunny and breezy, it being one of the most perfect summer days. The surrounding scenery, unsurpassed in its beautiful and picturesque features, added much to the charming interest of the occasion.

The place of meeting was a hill-side somewhat steep, from which there cropped out at different points rocky projections, affording natural and substantial platforms, which were occupied by musicians, juvenile singers, and speakers. At the foot of this terraced amphitheatre of nature's construction, tables were spread, tastefully ornamented with floral decorations, and richly loaded with refreshments. The best arrangements had been made to render the occasion both profitable and pleasant.

The assembly was called to order by Hon. JOHN A. ROCK-WELL, with a few remarks, when the following original Hymn, by Mrs. SIGOURNEY, was sung by the Sabbath School.

> Our ears have heard *their* righteous deeds
>   Which ancient records show,
> Who in this pleasant region dwelt
>   One hundred years ago.
>
> Their earnest care, their christian zeal
>   To guard with faithful hand
> The Church, the School, the Laws that make
>   The glory of our land.
>
> Oh! may the heavenly grace be ours
>   Now, in our early days
> Like them, to choose with love to walk
>   In our Redeemer's ways,
>
> That when to these delightful scenes
>   Our closing eyes grow dim,
> It also may of us be said,
>   They have gone home to Him.

Rev. Mr. HADEN, of Montville, offered prayer. Short addresses were made by the following gentlemen :—WILLIAM C.

GILMAN, Esq., of New York, the first Superintendent of the Sabbath School; Rev. JOSEPH HURLBUT, and Rev. G. B. WILcox, of New London ; WM. P. EATON, Esq., and Hon. L. F. S. FOSTER, of Norwich. Rev. Dr. BOND read extracts of letters from Mrs. SALLY DODGE, of New York, who united with this church sixty-six years ago,—and from Rev. WM. ALLEN, D. D., of Northampton, who forwarded an original Hymn for the occasion, which was read as follows :—

O Zion's KING ! Thee we adore,
    That here a hundred years ago,
On this unplanted river-shore
    A precious vine was made to grow.

Rich, clustering grapes from year to year,
    Which thou hast nourish'd in thy love,
Thy vine hath borne, and still doth bear,—
    Sweet foretaste of the joys above.

This CHURCH, O blest REDEEMER, still
    With every grace wilt thou endow,—
Thy Spirit every heart to fill
    With heaven's own bliss brought down below.

Thy CHURCH, O LORD, that growing vine,
    Shall spread its branches wide around,
Nurtur'd by Prayer, Truth, Power divine,
    Till knell of time on earth shall sound.

The venerable author of the foregoing Hymn, married for his second wife, Miss SARAH J. BREED, an esteemed member of this church. In a letter, dated. Northampton, July 10, 1860, he remarks in reply to one addressed to him,—" You are right in thinking, that, although shut up at home by severe illness, my heart will be with you then. Lying on my sofa, I write with a pencil a hymn designed to be adapted to your celebration."

The exercises of this occasion were interspersed with singing by the children of the Sabbath School, which was performed in a manner that reflected great credit on the teacher, who for several weeks had met them for the purpose of instruction in vocal music. When the sweet, tiny voices of the infant class were united in one of their spirited melodies, we were reminded of the words of inspiration,—" Out of the mouth of babes and sucklings hast thou ordained strength."

Two hours having been spent in these pleasant services, the chairman announced that the refreshments would now be distributed, which was received, especially by the juvenile portion of the assembly, with marked demonstrations of satisfaction. It was a charming spectacle to witness the elastic movements, the happy faces, and exuberant cheer of the many juvenile groups, that gathered round the tables, 'all borne with unconscious effort on a common tide of joyous, though controlled excitement. This scene in the programme having closed, the members of the school were re-called to their seats for the closing service. After a few remarks by the chairman, the following Hymn, composed by Mrs. S. P. Coit, was sung in the favorite tune, "Auld lang syne," in which the whole assembly united.

Now let us sing our parting song,
With these kind friends of ours,
For we have been a happy throng,
Among these leafy bowers.

We've heard of those good men, who laid
The first rough corner stone,
Of this dear church—God bless'd and made
Two spreading bands become.

Pastors who left this church for Heaven,
The flock fast following too,
Some who for heathen souls have striven,
How sweet, all to review!

Our fathers! Bless their memory for
Their century's holy work,
And on the coming hundred years,
We'll make our christian mark.

And now with very grateful hearts,
And very happy voice,
We'll bid these pleasant friends farewell,
Who've made us thus rejoice.

And when we've weathered storms and calms,
O'er life's rough ocean driven,
Through centuries long, may we adore
Our fathers' God,—in Heaven !

Thus the Centennial occasion was closed in a manner, satisfactory to all who had interested themselves in its arrangements. The day with its review of the past, and its hopes for the future, will form a historical epoch in the life of this church. The struggles of its infancy, through which it was carried, and the fruits of its manhood, which have abounded to the glory of God, are fitted to inspire the confidence, that, under the same good Shepherd it will be protected in all future emergencies, and, at the close of the century on which it has just entered, that a report will be made far richer in its recorded results, and a nobler jubilee celebrated.

The committee held a meeting, July 27th, when the report of the finance committee was heard and accepted.

A vote was adopted, requesting a copy of the discourse, delivered on the occasion, for publication.

The committee then finally adjourned.

F. A. DORRANCE, *Clerk.*

Note A.

The following is the Covenant, adopted at the time of the organization of the church :

Our Lord Jesus Christ, having finished the work of our redemption, and broken down the wall of partition between Jew and Gentile by removing the covenant of particularity out of the way, He has set up His own kingdom or church, and has sent His Gospel to all nations for the obedience of faith, and invited sinners of all nations to turn from dumb idols unto Him; and has required all who own Him to join together as opportunity may offer, into a particular society or church, to walk, worship, and serve Him agreeably to His blessed Gospel, and to watch over one another for their good, and not for their halting :

Wherefore, we, unworthy sinners, who have sometime lived without Christ and without God in the world, being now called out of it by the ministry of the Gospel, to the fellowship of Christ; and having our hearts stirred up by His Spirit, and made willing to join together in church state and communion, do by the help of Christ, renounce the devil, the wicked vain world, and the sinful lusts of the flesh, and all anti-christian pollutions, and our former evil ways; and do give up ourselves first to God, Father, Son, and Holy Ghost, through the mediation of Jesus Christ; we offer up our professed subjection to Jesus Christ, as the only Prophet, Priest, and King of His people, beseeching Him in His rich grace and free mercy to accept of us, as His covenant and peculiar people. And also we give up ourselves to one another by the will of God, promising, in the name and grace and strength of Christ, on whom we desire always to rely and trust, and who worketh in us both to will and to do, to worship God through Jesus Christ according to His commands, institutions, and appointments, as they do, or shall appear to be contained in the Word of God, and to watch over one another, and to walk together in brotherly love, according to the rules of the Gospel, to the common edification of the body and of each particular member, and to be guided in all things according to the revealed will of God, seeking to advance the glory of Jesus Christ our Head, both in church and brotherly communion, through the assistance of His Holy Spirit, which He has encouraged us to hope for by the Word of Truth; and to submit to the discipline of Christ in His church, and to maintain the worship of God in this place, while God shall continue us here; and we do consecrate and give up our children to Him, promising, by the help of His grace, to train them up in the nurture and admonition of the Lord, as God in His Word doth direct and require. And we do manifest our joint assent and consent herein, in the presence of the Lord and this assembly, by this our present public profession, and by setting or ordering to be set or affixed our names to this solemn covenant.

At the time of the formal and solemn renewing of their covenant, May 17th, 1787, a revised form was adopted, slightly differing from the foregoing, which is found on the records of the church, vol. I, pp. 48 and 49. The form, as adopted at this time, is, with a few verbal alterations, the same as that now used.

The Confession of Faith, adopted at the same time, is expressed in the following preamble and articles:

Whosoever will be saved, must confess with the mouth the Lord Jesus, and believe in his heart, that God hath raised Him from the dead; for with the heart man believeth unto righteousness, and with the mouth confession is made unto salvation. We do, therefore, from our hearts confess the faith of Christ, and profess to believe as follows:

I. There is one only living and true God, the unchangeable Jehovah, who is one in essence, yet subsisting as three persons, the Father, the Son, and the Holy Ghost.

II. That God did in the beginning create all things out of nothing by the word of His power, and by His will and providence preserves all creatures, ruling and governing them for His own glory.

III. God did create man in His image, after His own likeness, in knowledge, righteousness, and holiness; and therefore in a happy state, under a moral law, which was suitable for him, and a covenant of life, which was holy, reasonable, just and good.

IV. Man continued not in that estate; but our first parents (fell,) and we, and all mankind who descended from them by ordinary generation, did in, together, and with them, fall from that estate by sinning against God, and so are by nature the children of wrath, and liable to the pains of hell forever.

V. God has not left all mankind to perish in a state of sin and misery; but from all eternity elected some to everlasting life, and ordained to bring them into a state of salvation by a Redeemer.

VI. The Lord Jesus Christ, who is both God and man, two distinct natures in one person, by a wonderful conception and incarnation in the womb of the blessed virgin Mary, through the power of the Holy Ghost, is the only Redeemer of God's elect, who has offered up Himself in His death a propitiatory sacrifice to God, and purchased everlasting salvation for them.

VII. The Holy and Eternal Spirit of God, whose special work it is to apply the redemption purchased by Christ to the souls of men, doth by working faith in us, unite us to Christ, and make us effectual partakers of the saving benefits of the death of Christ, insomuch that they, who do believe on His name, are justified.

VIII. God requires of us and of all Christians, as necessary duties, though not meritorious conditions of eternal life, faith in our Lord Jesus Christ, repentance towards God, and sincere and unfeigned holiness in heart and life, with a diligent use of all the means, appointed for the application of the benefits of redemption, which are, especially His Word, contained in the Scriptures of the Old and New Testaments, and Prayer to God in the name of Christ, the only Mediator, together with the sacraments of the new Covenant, Baptism and the Lord's Supper.

IX. There will be a resurrection of the dead bodies, both of the just and unjust, and a reunion of the soul and body, so that they shall be jointly and together, capable of being the subjects of happiness, or of misery to all eternity.

X. There will be a great and general Judgment, God having appointed a day in which he will judge the world by Jesus Christ, whereof he hath in the Gospel given assurance to all men; and at the last day, the Son of Man shall come from Heaven in the glory of the Father, attended with his Holy Angels, and sitting on a throne of glory, before him shall be gathered all nations, and he shall judge the world in righteousness; the sum of which judgment will be, that the wicked shall go away into everlasting punishment, and the righteous into life eternal.

This confession was publicly read, and assented to by those who signed the Covenant on the 24th of July, 1760.

MINISTER'S PEW.

FREE SEAT FOR AGED WOMEN.

FREE SEAT FOR AGED MEN.

STAIRS.

FRONT.

STAIRS.

The dimensions of the building were forty-one by thirty-seven feet. The Plan here given, is drawn from memoranda, furnished some years since by SYLVESTER HILL, Esq.

The Articles of Faith with the Scripture proofs, and the Church Covenant, in their present form, were adopted by the Church, July 27, 1829, and first printed with a Catalogue, in 1830. The number on this Catalogue is 177, of whom 22 only remain.

Note B.

The following are the names of the pew-holders, two families being accommodated in the same pew, as follows :

Seth Harding and William Rockwell ; Sybile Crocker and Jonathan Lester ; Thomas Trapp, Jr., and Stephen Barker ; Jabez Dean and Elijah Lathrop ; John Tracy and Peter Lanman ; Joseph Trumbull and Jabez Perkins ; Ephraim Bill and Hugh Ledlie : Ebenezer Fillmore, Jr., and Timothy Herrick ; William Coit and Simon Carew ; Nathaniel Backus and Nathaniel Backus, Jr. ; Abel Brewster and John Martin ; David Lamb and Moses Pierce ; Benajah Leffingwell and Ezra Backus ; Benjamin Huntington and Nathaniel Shipman ; Joseph Smith and Isaac Park ; Stephen Roath and Stephen Roath, Jr. ; Hannah Wight and Joseph Kelley ; Jacob DeWitt and John M'Clarren Breed ; John and Peter Waterman ; Benjamin and George Dennis ; Caleb Whitney and Joshua Norman ; Daniel Kelley and William Capron ; Prosper Wetmore and Ebenezer Fitch ; David Roath and Samuel Roath ; William Breed and Zephaniah Jennings ; Joseph Wight and Lemuel Buswell. The minister and his family had the use of an entire pew assigned to them. Fifty-two pew-holders besides the family of the minister, are included in this record, as it appears on the Society's books.

Note C.

The mission of Dr. WHITAKER in behalf of the "Indian Charity School," identifies him and this church with the work of missions in a manner worthy of remark. The successful labors of DAVID BRAINARD among the Indians about that time, had awakened in the churches much interest for the conversion and civilization of the native inhabitants. The proximity of the Mohegan tribe, and their firm frendship, created a missionary spirit in the older church of this town, in which our church and its Pastor participated. A mission school for Indian youth was founded by Rev. ELEAZER WHEELOCK, at Lebanon. It was patronized by the General Court of Massachusetts, which assumed for a time the support of six Indian youth. The General Assembly of New Hampshire made a donation to promote the design. Contributions were sent in from churches and individuals. Among the benefactors were Rev. GEORGE WHITEFIELD, the COUNTESS of HUNTINGTON, and other foreigners.

SAMSON OCCUM was one of the first pupils of this school, and as he became a preacher of popular talents, it was arranged for him to go on an agency for it to the mother country, accompanied by Dr. WHITAKER. This mission was so successful, as to justify an enlargement of the plan, and, as the result, the Indian Charity School became the foundation of DARTMOUTH COLLEGE. The missionary zeal of Dr. WHITAKER was an element in his life and ministry, which for those times entitles him to be reckoned as one of the honored pioneers in the work of evangelizing the pagan tribes of this new world. And the fact is not without interest, that his labors were subsequently identified with the Tabernacle church in Salem, Mass., in which at a later period, the Rev. Dr. WORCESTER, one of the founders, and the first Secretary of the American Board of Foreign Missions, officiated as Pastor till his death.

The facts, to which this reference is made, unimportant as they may seem in the eventful history of missions in our country, may be regarded as constituting one of the small head-springs, whence there has arisen a noble tributary to that river of missionary influences and agencies, which is diffusing the waters of life over the arid wastes of the heathen world. Thus to trace a noble stream up to its source in some hidden spring, while pleasing to the historic inquirer, affords an instructive illustration of the method, in which Divine Providence works in the incipiency and development of its plans.

Note D.

FORM OF A "SISTERLY COVENANT" ADOPTED IN THE YEAR 1790.

We, whose names are here written, having, as we hope, a sincere desire for the glory of God, and the good of our own souls and others, have thought proper, besides the Covenant we have already made with God and each other, to make this also, whereby we hope mutually to assist each other in our Christian course.

1. We think it best to set apart one evening of every week, for the purpose of meeting together to read the Holy Scriptures, and other good books, to sing the praises of our Redeemer, but more especially to pray with and for each other, for our dear friends, and all our fellow creatures.

2. We propose to begin our meetings at the time of lighting candles, and not be needlessly absent, but must be as near the time as we can ; read while our company is collecting, then begin with prayer, then sing a hymn, or psalm, next we may read in the Bible, and converse, if we think proper, till it is time to conclude with prayer and singing.

3. Every member that agrees to take her turn in the performance, is to do it in the order of her name, as annexed to this our agreement, and in case the person should be absent, whose turn it is to pray, the next in order must do it in her stead, and the absent one must perform the next time. It is agreed that no person shall be urged to perform this duty against her will ; but it is hoped, that none will long refuse, since God looks only on the heart.

4. We promise not to divulge the infirmities of a fellow member, but to keep all things secret belonging to the Society, the discovery of which might be a disadvantage.

5. We resolve to be charitable to each other, and to advise, caution, admonish one another, and we agree not to be offended, but kindly and thankful-

ly receive reproof from any of our members. We shall endeavor that our discourse while together, shall be of the things that pertain to godliness. And when apart, our behavior shall be such as becomes Christianity. And if any member commits any offence, and after being often reproved, still continues impenitent, she shall be excluded from us, until she gives evidence of her sorrow for her past conduct.

6. We further agree, that if any person desires to join with us, it shall be mentioned in one of our meetings, and the one chosen for our head shall converse with her, and if there be no objection, she shall be orderly received as a member.

Signed,

ANNA BUSWELL,	EUNICE HART,
SARAH LANMAN,	LYDIA M'CURDY,
SARAH TRAPP,	BETSEY BREED,
LYDIA PERKINS,	SALLY DODGE,
SARAH SMITH,	LYDIA BREED,
HANNAH JOHNSON,	MARTHA WILLIAMS,
ABIGAIL YOUNG,	ELIZABETH BUSWELL,
SARAH KING,	MARY HUNTINGTON,
SUSANNA HOWLAND,	MARY ANNA G. LANMAN,
ANNA VERA KIRTLAND,	REBECCA BREED,
ANNA FANNING,	SARAH PERKINS,
ANNA COIT,	REBECCA HUNTINGTON,
MARY SILSBY,	SALLY HUNTINGTON,
LUCINDA CHENEY,	BETSEY PERKINS,
ELIZABETH HUNTINGTON,	ABIGAIL WILLIAMS,
PERCY PEABODY,	ELIZABETH GREEN,
ANNA REDDY,	BETSEY ROCKWELL,
ELIZABETH ROCKWELL,	NANCY COIT,
CATHERINE PEABODY,	SARAH DEMING.

Note E.

CIRCULAR AND CONSTITUTION OF THE FIRST FOREIGN MISSIONARY SOCIETY.

The period in which we live, is deeply interesting to the Church and to the world. While the Most High is arising to shake terribly the earth, and to punish the inhabitants for their iniquities, he is not unmindful of his own cause. The last fifteen years have not been more distinguished as a season of distress and perplexity to the nations of the earth, than for the exertions, to which many are awakened, for the spread and establishment of the Redeemer's kingdom through the world. Among such exertions none are more animating, and worthy of support, than those which are directed to translation of the Holy Scriptures into the languages of many benighted millions, and the sending of able and pious missionaries to instruct them in the way of eternal life.

* * * * * * * *

Under the direction of a respectable Board of Commissioners of five gentlemen in Massachusetts, and four in this State, five young men of the most promising character have already taken their departure, as missionaries to the East Indies. Several others are preparing to follow them ; while many societies are forming for their support, and for promoting the benevolent object of their mission, by aiding the translation of the Scriptures.

In these labors of love to the Redeemer, and to the souls of our fellow men, we are desirous to bear a part. In proportion as we value the precious privileges, which God has graciously bestowed on our ancestors, and on us, we would cheerfully acknowledge the duty of extending the same privileges to those who have never seen a Bible, nor heard the name of a Savior. While we consider, the earth is " the Lord's and the fulness thereof," that the silver and the gold are his, and that we are stewards for him of all we possess, we would cheerfully contribute of our substance for promoting the glory of the Redeemer in the instruction and salvation of our fellow sinners.

With such impression, and such views of this momentous subject—we, the subscribers, do hereby associate for the purposes here contemplated, and give our consent to the following

CONSTITUTION.

ARTICLE 1. The name of this Association shall be THE FOREIGN MISSION SOCIETY OF NORWICH AND THE VICINITY.

2. The general object of the Society shall be to raise money for the support of Foreign Missions, and to aid the translation of the Bible into various languages,—the particular objects being specified in the subscription.

3. Every person who shall subscribe to this Constitution, and shall engage to pay to the Treasurer of this Society annually a sum not less than one dollar, shall be a member.

4. Every person paying fifty dollars at one time, shall be a member of the Society for life.

5. The officers of the Society shall be a President, Vice Presidents, a Secretary, Treasurer, and Auditor, to be chosen by ballot at the annual meeting.

6. The Society shall hold its annual meeting, alternately in the first and second Society in Norwich, on the third Tuesday of May in each year.

7. The first payment shall be made at or before the first annual meeting.

8. Defines the duties of the Secretary.

9. Defines the duties of the Treasurer.

10. The Society will receive donations for the support of either of the above (named) purposes, under such restrictions as the donors shall impose, and will pay such donations according to the direction of the donors.

11. Defines the mode in which the current expenses of the Society shall be met.

12. If the office of the Secretary or Treasurer shall become vacant during the year, the President shall designate a person to fill his place.

13. Any member may withdraw from this Society by giving written notice to the Treasurer of his intention to withdraw, and paying all arrearages.

14. No alteration shall be made in this Constitution, unless by a vote of two-thirds of the members, present at an annual meeting.

OFFICERS OF THE SOCIETY.

Rev. JOSEPH STRONG, D. D., President.

Rev. ASAHEL HOOKER,
ZECHARIAH HUNTINGTON, Esq., } Vice Presidents.

JABEZ HUNTINGTON, Esq., Secretary.

HEZEKIAH PERKINS, Esq., Treasurer.

JAMES STEDMAN, Esq., Auditor.

NORWICH, May 25, 1812.

In this record we recognize one of the first auxiliary Missionary Societies organized in the country. From the commencement of its operations it has not failed to contribute annually to the funds of the American Board. The Foreign Missionary Society of New London and vicinity, was organized April 14, 1812. Gen. JEDEDIAH HUNTINGTON, the grand-father of Mrs. ELI SMITH, was the first President of the Society. In the month of June following, the sum total for Foreign Missions, acknowledged in the Panoplist, was $1379 15 ; of which amount $375 60 was contributed by the two Societies, principally that of New London and vicinity. During the first year they forwarded $531 60, to the Treasurer of the Board of Missions. A few years since, these Societies were united under the name of "Norwich and New London Foreign Missionary Society."

Note F.

The native place of the present Pastor was Sutton, Mass. He was graduated at Brown University, in 1815. His theological studies were prosecuted at the Theological Seminary, Andover, Mass., where he remained as a resident graduate most of the year after having completed the regular course of study. Near the close of that year, 1819, he was ordained and installed as Pastor of the Congregational Church in Sturbridge. Having prosecuted his labors there about ten years, he accepted an appointment, as Professor of Sacred Literature, in the Theological Seminary, Bangor, Maine. The severity of the climate affecting his health unfavorably, he was induced to seek a field of labor in a milder region. In the winter of 1835, an invitation from this Church and Society was extended to him to assume the pastorate thereof, which was accepted.

On the sixth of May the following Council was convened to attend to the, preliminary services, and perform the solemnities of the installation.

Rev. SAMUEL NOTT, D.D., Franklin;	ASHBEL WOODWARD, Delegate.
" LEVI NELSON, Lisbon;	FREEMAN TRACY, "
" LYMAN STRONG, Colchester;	R. H. ISHAM, "
" TIMOTHY TUTTLE, Ledyard;	ISAAC GALLUP, "
" JOEL HAWES, D. D., Hartford;	WILLIAM WATSON, "
" CHARLES HYDE, Norwich; (without charge.)	
" JOEL W. NEWTON, Norwich;	WM. C. GILMAN, Delegate.
" A. B. COLLINS, Preston;	GEORGE LORING, "
Fourth Church, Norwich.	S. L. HOUGH, "

The Rev. Mr. STRONG presided as Moderator, and Rev. CHAS. HYDE acted Scribe. The sermon on the occasion was preached by Dr. HAWES. The installing prayer was offered by Dr. NOTT. The charge was addressed to the Pastor by Mr. STRONG. The Right Hand of Fellowship was given by Mr. NEWTON.

Note G.

The edifice, which at present is occupied as the house of worship by the Second Congregational Church, is ninety-one feet in length, including the tower, and sixty-four feet in width. It contains one hundred and twenty slips on the floor, and twenty-four in the gallery, besides the orchestra. The architecture is of the Roman order, the plan of which was furnished by a professional architect, Mr. WARREN, of Providence, R. I. The building Committee were Messrs. RUSSELL HUBBARD, WILLIAM WILLIAMS, CHARLES W. ROCKWELL, GEORGE PERKINS, DANIEL L. TRUMBULL and HENRY ALLEN.

The services of dedication consisted in reading selections of Scripture by Rev. ELI SMITH, Missionary from Beirut, introductory prayer by the venerable SAMUEL NOTT, D. D., in the ninety-second year of his age; sermon by the Pastor; dedicatory prayer by Rev. THOMAS L. SHIPMAN; concluding prayer by Rev. Mr. CLARK, Pastor of the Central Baptist Church, whose house of worship had been kindly offered for the use of the Society, while their house was in the progress of building.

The resident members of the Church at this time numbered two hundred and eighty. The Deacons were JABEZ HUNTINGTON, JOSEPH OTIS, H. B. BUCKINGHAM and CHARLES COIT.

The organ, which cost about three thousand dollars, was the gift of Dea. JOSEPH OTIS, who, in addition to many other liberal benefactions, founded and endowed the Library, which bears his name. Besides this, he contributed one thousand dollars towards the establishment of the Pastor's Library. A rich silver christening vase was presented to the Church by Mrs. EUNICE B. FARNSWORTH, and a plated communion service with a silver cup was given by Miss MARY R. MACKIE, now Mrs. FRANK JOHNSON. A beautiful Bible for the pulpit was presented by CHARLES BOSWELL, of Hartford.

In the summer of 1855, this house of worship underwent extensive repairs, and important changes, at an expense of about six thousand dollars. This amount was subscribed and promptly paid when the work was done. The dimensions of the Church are sufficient to accommodate eight hundred hearers, and with extra seats a thousand persons may be comfortably seated.

The Sabbath School room is fifty-nine feet by thirty-six, exclusive of the room for the infant class, and will accommodate from three hundred and fifty to four hundred scholars. The Lecture room contains seats for one hundred and seventy-five. All these rooms have been furnished so as to make them comfortable and pleasant.

Note H.

The persons referred to, as having entered into the work of the Gospel Ministry from the Sabbath School, are the following:

L. D. BENTLEY,	SILAS H. HAZZARD,
ALBERT T. CHESTER,	WALTER K. WILKIE,
HENRY BROMLEY,	DANIEL W. HAVENS,
EDWARD W. GILMAN,	JAMES A. BOLLES,
ELIAS B. HILLARD,	WILLIAM PALMER,
GILES B. WILCOX,	JOHN T. COIT,
WILLIAM TRACY,	FRANCIS C. WOODWORTH,
CHARLES H. CHESTER,	TIMOTHY DWIGHT,
JAMES DWIGHT,	HENRY D. WOODWORTH.

Several have died while preparing for the ministry, viz:—PETER L. HUNTINGTON, JOHN B. DWIGHT, DANIEL WILLES, and N. W. DEWEY.

Note I.

The following catalogue of Missionaries, who have gone from the original limits embraced in the Town of Norwich, was prepared by WILLIAM C. GILMAN, Esq., once a member of this Church, now of New York.

Year.	Names.	Mission.
1761.	Rev. SAMSON OCCUM. - - - - -	Oneida.
1766.	" SAMUEL KIRTLAND, - - - -	"
1812.	" SAMUEL NOTT, JR. - - - - -	Mahratta.
1812.	Mrs. NOTT, (Roxana Peck,) - - - -	"
1819.	Rev. MIRON WINSLOW, - - - - -	Ceylon.
1819.	Mrs. WINSLOW, (Harriet Lathrop,) - -	"
1821.	Rev. WILLIAM POTTER, - - - - -	Cherokee.
1825.	Mr. WILLIAM H. MANWARING, - , - -	"
1826.	Mrs. ANSON GLEASON, (B. W. Tracy.) - -	Choctaw.
1827.	Rev. JONATHAN S. GREEN, - -	Sandwich Islands.
1827.	Mrs. GULIC, (Fanny H. Thomas,) - - -	"
1833.	Mrs. ELY SMITH, (Sarah L. Huntington,) - -	Syria.
1833.	Mrs. PALMER, (Jerusha Johnson,) - - -	Cherokee.
1833.	Mrs. HUTCHINS, (Elizabeth C. Lathrop,) - -	Ceylon.
1833.	Mrs. PERRY, (Harriet L. Lathrop,) - - - -	"
1833.	Rev. STEPHEN JOHNSON, - - - - -	Siam.
1835.	" JAMES T. DICKINSON, - - - - -	Singapore.
1835.	" WILLIAM TRACY, - - - - -	Madura.
1835.	Mrs. HEBARD, (Rebecca W. Williams,) - -	Syria.
1836.	Mrs. CHERRY, (Charlotte H. Lathrop,) - -	Madura.
1836.	Rev. JAMES L. THOMPSON, - - - - -	Cyprus.
1839.	Mrs. PALMER, (Clarissa Johnson,) - - -	Cherokee.
1839.	Mrs. SHERMAN, (Martha E. Williams,) - -	Syria.

1839.	Mrs. Brewer, (Laura L. Giddings,)	-	-	Oregon.
1840.	Rev. Joshua Smith, - - - - -			Africa.
1844.	Miss Susan Tracy, - - - - - -			Choetaw.
1844.	" Lucinda Downer, - - - - -			"
	" Eunice Starr, - - - - -			"
1854.	Rev. William Aitchison, - - - -			China.
1860.	" Wm. F. Arms, - - - -			Bulgaria.

Fourteen Missions have been or are at present strengthened and sustained by the sons and daughters of the Congregational Churches of Norwich, as it was one hundred years ago. This fact has, as would be naturally expected, created in these Churches a healthy and stable interest in the work of Foreign Missions—an interest that lives in unabated vigor and efficiency.